D1546067

TRAPPED IN THE
FAMILY BUSINESS®

ISBN: 0984949216
ISBN 13: 9780984949212
MK Insights LLC, Northampton, MA

CHAPTERS

MANY THANKS TO...

...the many individuals who chose to share their personal family business stories with me.

...those advisors and other business professionals whom I am proud to call colleagues and friends.

...two very special professionals who nurtured and supported my early work in the family business arena: Ira Bryck and Tom Waring Jr.

...two important people in my life who I am incredibly proud to be related to: Henry Klein and Benjamin Klein.

...my father, Robert M. Klein, CLU, ChFC, (1933-2017).

SECOND EDITION
INTRODUCTION

Since first publishing *TFB* in 2012, I have heard from, spoken to, and met with people who have helped me understand that you can feel trapped at any stage in your career in a family business; whether they were in their early twenties and unsure of their career trajectory; in their mid-forties and reevaluating their work and relationships; or in their sixties or seventies, and concerned about exiting because the next generation was not yet ready to take over. Despite different perspectives, they all shared a desire to follow their own path while maintaining and respecting those familial relationships that were held in high regard. This edition attempts to highlight that commonality by focusing on two key elements that every family business member should always keep in mind, and in balance (chapter VI).

Over the past six years, I have also connected with parents who want their children to see the family business as a wonderful opportunity rather than an obligation or trap. Some of these parents were founders and knew little about next generation engagement and transition, while others wanted to avoid their own negative (or often, overly controlled) experience of entering the business. I have included generally agreed upon practices as well as my own observations of successful family business parenting strategies in chapter VII.

Another addition can be found at the back of the book: "Exploration: Key Questions." Think of this resource as a self-guided process that ties into Chapter IV and provides specific ways to uncover information that will guide action when facing challenging situations related to family business entry and exit.

Something that has become clear to me since first writing *TFB* is that it is <u>absolutely</u> possible to not only manage trapped situations, but that they can be avoided. I have seen family enterprises where it is abundantly clear and widely acknowledged that the business has provided unique and joyful opportunities, careers, and personal experiences that would not have been found elsewhere. However, it cannot be overstated that the price of admission will always include extra effort, significant thought, and more than a few challenging conversations.

Michael Klein, PsyD
Northampton, Massachusetts
April 2018
Michael@trappedinthefamilybusiness.com

FOREWORD

Early one Monday morning a few years back, I received an urgent call from a colleague and friend, Mark. Mark is a financial advisor in Philadelphia, and he was concerned that one of his clients was about to make some very abrupt, life-changing decisions.

This client, a thirty-something business owner, had called Mark late Sunday night and asked him to start the paperwork to get him out of the family business as soon as humanly possible. He had had enough.

"Hold on," Mark told his client, Stephen. "Before you make any decisions you might regret, you need to at least talk with a colleague of mine."

The subsequent conversation I had with Stephen marked the beginning of an idea that has resulted in this book. After working with him, I found myself consulting with, and coaching, others just like him.

These were individuals who were frustrated with their family business situations, were emotionally burned out, and didn't have a clue as to what should (and could) be done about it.

As soon as I started calling this particular situation "Trapped in the Family Business," the floodgates opened, and I found myself talking to countless people in family businesses who were very much aware of this phenomenon, either in themselves or in others.

And they had found no resources for their seemingly unique and complicated situation.

Of course, as it turns out, this situation is far from unique—though it is quite complicated.

While researching this topic, I conducted over thirty interviews with family business members, consultants, academics, and writers. They all agreed that this scenario is increasingly common among family businesses and has been around as long as anyone can remember; one experienced family business advisor suggested, somewhat lightheartedly, that somewhere between 95 and 99 percent of the people he has worked with have felt trapped in their family business at some point.

My hope is that this book assists those who are trapped to:

1. *Realize how widespread this situation is*
2. *Enhance their understanding of how they got there*
3. *Create a road map for moving forward*
4. *Free themselves from being, and feeling, trapped*

For friends, colleagues, families, and advisors, perhaps this book will increase your understanding (and empathy) for this situation and provide a way for you to offer support.

I have also included information and links at the end of this book, including Trapped in the Family Business® roundtables, retreats and more.

Finally, please don't keep this book a secret from those who may benefit from reading it. Simply knowing that other people share, and understand, a difficult situation can be the first step in doing something about it.

Michael Klein, PsyD
Northampton, Massachusetts
April 2012

Every emotional unit, whether it be the family or the total of society, exerts pressure on group members to conform to the ideals and principals of the group.

- Murray Bowen (1976)

CHAPTER I

TRAPPED?

If you do not have direct experience in a family business, you probably don't know what it feels like, or maybe how it is even possible, to be trapped in a family business.

"How can you be *trapped?*" you might ask. "You don't have a 'real' boss and you can make your own hours. You might even have ownership in the company (now or in the future) and you have more power than a regular employee. You get to work with people you care about, you get to contribute to something that is bigger than any one person, and your name is even on the door!"

To borrow a term from the corporate world, feeling trapped in any business can be caused by possessing "golden handcuffs." These handcuffs are typically financial and other incentives to keep an employee from leaving the company (e.g., stock options, etc., that won't be accessible if the employee leaves).

For those feeling trapped in a family business, however, "emotional handcuffs" may be a more relevant term. Guilt, obligation, history, legacy—all of these can play a role in bringing someone into the family business and keeping him or her there.

In addition to this, all of the perceived benefits of being in a family business can also have a downside. Having your name on the door translates to not being able to ever *really* take time off (you are always "on call" in one way or another). Family business also comes with its own burdens of protecting and growing the company for future generations, not to mention for the sake of those who have come before.

Autonomy (i.e., being one's own boss, making one's own schedule) often comes with the price of filling many different roles as needed, resulting in a general lack of clear (and written) job responsibilities.

One of the originators of psychoanalysis, Sigmund Freud, believed that growing up brings with it a more realistic and objective view of reality—one in which there are two sides to every story, and where adults must learn to balance impulsivity with thoughtful planning. This book holds the same philosophy.

For those trapped in the family business, it is important to develop a realistic and objective view of their situation. Although there may be an intense desire to take action immediately, it is much more advisable to take a thorough, objective, and honest look at the situation and potential next steps.

TIM: BROTHERS IN ARMS

Tim and his older brother, Mark, had worked in the family business since they were kids. The logistics company their father started had grown from a basement business to a $15-million-a-year company.

When they were in their midtwenties, as their father was eyeing retirement, they arranged to buy him out. Both brothers had been waiting eagerly for this moment since they were teenagers. After their mother died, the boys and their father had become very close, and the business was a great source of connection for them.

Tim and Mark worked side by side for many years, and both were thrilled to finally take control and fully implement their own strategies and ideas. Their father was pleased as well, as he had not been sure the boys would be interested enough to make such a major financial commitment.

The plan went forward, they agreed on a selling price and buyout plan, and everyone was happy. Mark would own 55 percent and Tim 45 percent, due to the amount of time they had each worked in the company.

A few years came and went, they weren't hitting their financial goals, and something started to change. While the brothers had initially thought that working together would continue to be comfortable and relatively harmonious, now that the business was struggling, they began to develop very different ideas about what should come next. They outlined conflicting strategies about how best to get back "in the black."

Tension in their relationship started to become unbearable. In addition, Tim's role was wearing on him, while Mark had become quite an expert in his area of the business.

Tim's increasing dissatisfaction in his job, coupled with Mark's increasingly controlling and bottom-line orientation to work, was taking a toll emotionally and physically. The brothers were having loud arguments almost daily, avoiding each other outside of work, and losing their ability to communicate without someone getting offended or furious.

Tim started having physical symptoms: first stomachaches, then back pain, then the inability to work full days. He developed high blood pressure, and his doctor told him something had to change or his twin eighteen-month-old sons were going to be living without a father.

CHAPTER II

BEGINNINGS:
HOW DOES IT HAPPEN?

Although nobody is born trapped in the family business, the seeds are often planted well before birth. Imagine the parent who thinks "having a family business will not only provide financial resources for my children, but also a job, a purpose, and prestige." Those children already have their careers mapped out, complete with job, goals, and industry.

In some ways, working in the family business can be remarkably similar to being in an arranged marriage. There are many parts of the world (whether geographically or culturally) where it is understood and accepted that parents will choose their child's mate. Elsewhere, the idea of an arranged marriage is highly unusual—the very concept may even be considered unfair and outdated.

Just as the tradition of arranged marriage has died out in many cultures, it is very likely that many will someday see "arranged occupations"—whereby parents control a child's career path or job through employment in the family business—as old-fashioned, unjust, and inexcusable.

Through working with clients and conducting numerous interviews, I have identified twelve dynamics that explain how and why individuals can become, and remain, trapped in a family business. More than one dynamic is typically involved.

Each of the following sections includes comments from *real people* who were, or still are, trapped in their family business.

☑ GUILT & OBLIGATION

"I just can't imagine being a part of this family without working in the business."

Family dynamics are complex, and it can take years of study to fully understand them. However, what is abundantly clear is that guilt and obligation often run deep in family business situations.

People who are trapped often feel an overwhelming sense of personal responsibility to the family and the business that prevents them from even thinking about changing their situation.

Guilt and obligation can arise from a direct concern for those who would be "left behind" or a general sense of indebtedness.

The potential feelings of remorse might be so painful that no change is entertained in the slightest. For example, it might be too difficult to imagine the struggle of family members and/or employees if the trapped individual were to leave. What if the business were even to fail?

Or maybe exceptional financial or professional opportunities and benefits provided by the family business have led to a strong sense of obligation.

Whether they are felt because of direct and explicit messages from others, or subtle and implied ones, guilt and obligation can be powerful motivators to maintain the status quo.

Also worthy of note, guilt and obligation are among the principal reasons why trapped family business members can be at odds with their spouses. Put simply, spouses don't have the history or connection to the family or business that the family member does. Yet a spouse can often more clearly perceive the high price that a husband or wife is paying by remaining in the business because of these all-too-common feelings of guilt or obligation. To the family member, this can be much more challenging to recognize.

☑ GUILT & OBLIGATION

"I'm here because if this business goes under, my parents will have nothing, and I couldn't live with that."

"My brother would have no idea how to do what I do."

"The only reason Dad paid for college was so I could help out in the business once I was done."

"After my father passed away, my mother was in a crunch, so I needed to help out."

"Not to be arrogant, but without me, I would worry about what would happen, especially to all the employees who have given their lives to this business."

"It would kill my parents if I left."

☑ PARENTAL LOVE

*"I needed a job after college and had no idea what
I wanted. So my parents created a job for me."*

Parents often see a job opportunity in the family business as a way to provide support, assistance, and money. They also consider it an indirect (or direct) expression of their love. Unfortunately, this is often a blind spot for parents, as working in the family business can have long-term negative consequences.

One of the most difficult parts of parenting can be letting children fail. Wanting to help one's child avoid pain or mistakes is perfectly natural and normal, but overly shielding a child from the outside world can also cause significant problems later on.

While children may be protected from the pain or potential failure that comes with striking out on their own, it also denies them the satisfaction, learning, and personal identity that accompany making one's own way in life. This troubling situation becomes even more harmful when children fail to see their own dependence on parents as a problem.

In addition, parents' desires to avoid their own anxiety or concerns may *unintentionally* cause them to shield their children. For example, what happens if a child gets hurt? Would it also somehow imply that they are bad parents? Or, if a child fails, does that mean that the parents have inadequately prepared them? What if a child achieves *more* than his or her parents?

Imagine that, by watching their children go out into the world and succeed, parents are forced to confront the reality that they too might have had a different, and perhaps more satisfying, career path elsewhere.

It is important to understand that this is not an "either/or" situation. Parents may be attempting to protect themselves *as well as* their child (or children) from what might happen outside of the family business.

☑ PARENTAL LOVE

"In hindsight, I think they decided working in the family business was the best for me. I never had to compete with anybody, really, or hit any definite goals. The job was just always there for me."

"After I got laid off, I couldn't find work. I needed a job, so they found one for me (in the business). They just said that's what parents do."

"They would tell me about cousins who got other jobs and didn't like them, or had terrible bosses, or something else that went wrong, and how I could avoid that whole ugliness by just coming into the family business."

☑ PROTECTION OF PARENTS

*"I couldn't stand to watch Dad get ripped
off by vendors."*

Although, by definition, one of the roles of parents is to protect their children, the opposite is often the case—and this unquestionably happens in family businesses. Roles are reversed and a child becomes the protector of his or her own parent(s).

This is certainly a struggle for anyone dealing with aging parents, as an example. In family businesses, however, it can be tricky because there are ownership and supervisory issues that are directly related to parental capacity. Often, because of the many implications, these issues are avoided for far too long.

In addition, children who become better educated than their parents might feel the need to join and remain in the family business. These individuals see their advanced education as a compelling reason to work or stay in the business: to share the skills and knowledge from their own education with their parents.

Depending on the state of the family business, the parents' potential lack of certain skills, and the child's abilities, this type of offer can be tough for a parent to refuse. As time goes by, and the child or children become more and more integral to the business, plans for different careers or job paths get further and further away.

☑ **PROTECTION OF PARENTS**

"Dad shows no signs of leaving—I don't think he thinks he'll ever die—and I'm not going to be the one to tell him it's time to go."

"I don't want them to think I don't want to be a member of the family or that I don't care about the business or think their life's work is not meaningful/important."

"Dad was falling behind the times and didn't know about new production methods and technology, and I could help."

☑ FAMILY LEGACY

"Joining the family business was just what was right. It wasn't about figuring out what you wanted, or what you were good at, or what made you happy. My family considered that selfish."

In long-standing, multigenerational family businesses, "legacy" can become a dirty word; it can feel like a domineering boss who micromanages your life, or even an oppressive dictator who demands complete loyalty and compliance.

In these situations, the individual becomes nothing more than a servant to the family name, the family business, and the legacy of every previous family member who poured his or her heart and soul into the business.

Parents, who may want to simply sustain the family legacy, can unintentionally overemphasize the importance of the continuity of the family business—especially when this is exactly what their own parents communicated to them. The business, and the family name, becomes far more important than anything a single individual may want or need.

And to consider, or act, outside of this expectation can seem unthinkable.

☑ FAMILY LEGACY

"This is what all the children have always been expected to do. There really wasn't a choice."

"It's just what you did. Some (kids) went to college and found some job in finance or with some charity. I went right into the family business. (I) always knew I would—for the business and the family name and reputation."

"I learned from a very young age that being born into this family means you are born with certain responsibilities. My father was taught this, his father was taught this, and his father. We all learn that the family is much greater than any one person, and we each have to do our part."

☑ EGO (PRIDE)

*"Someday they will understand how important
I was to this business."*

Self-image (how people view themselves and perceive their own abilities) can be based on many different things. For some, it's all about others acknowledging their skills, talents, or value.

In family businesses, this can translate to family members staying in the business simply to show a parent or some other relative that they are important or can achieve something significant. Family members might also stay to demonstrate that they can do something nobody else thought they were capable of.

For others, staying in the family business may be about avoiding the fact they are not as important (or central) to the running of the business as they think they are. What if they leave and the business doesn't even experience a hiccup? What if the business works *more* effectively without them? Either of these would be a very difficult and painful truth to confront.

Regardless of the exact reason, in these cases, showing or proving their value to others becomes more important than their own professional satisfaction, long-term goals, or, in many cases, a fulfilling relationship with a spouse and their own children.

☑ EGO (PRIDE)

"I needed to prove to my parents that they were wrong about me—that I *could* run the business and be successful."

"I put in so much time—I refuse to leave with my tail between my legs."

"I wanted to show them they were right—that I was able to take the business to the next level."

"Dad assumed my brother would work (in the family business) and that I wouldn't—or maybe couldn't."

☑ COMFORT

*"I've spent all my free time since I could
remember working in the family business.
It just always felt comfortable."*

For so many, their role in the family business is comfortable and easy—free from major problems and without much pressure, if any.

For these individuals, the job may have been created just for them—or they were put in a leadership role and told just to "keep things going"—or a parent may have given them a responsibility that was not particularly difficult or challenging.

After a while, it can become difficult to imagine working elsewhere, much less having to go through a job search (for the first time!), working for someone they don't like, or not being able to make their own work schedule. Even if they do venture out, the stress and anxiety they suddenly confront may push them right back into the family business. Incredibly, for some, there can even be great comfort in family business quarrels and disagreements if this is what is most familiar.

Unfortunately, too much comfort, or a lack of challenge, will result in little development or growth. And if working in the family business has been the only job experience, staying comfortable in the family business just reinforces one's identity as the boss's son or daughter—not an independent and autonomous adult.

☑ COMFORT

"It seemed like an easy path."

"I wasn't getting anywhere in my other job, so this was easy to fall back on."

"I didn't really have any choices when I graduated—so I came here, mostly because I knew the people and what went on."

"I became addicted to the ups and downs, the arguments, the conflict. I couldn't imagine doing a job without constant family disputes—how boring would that be?"

☑ SEDUCTION

*"I had the typical thought: someday all of
this will be mine."*

There are many ways that parents can, and have, unintentionally trapped their children in the business by painting a picture of a phenomenal future. Parents can focus exclusively on the advantages of being in a family business while ignoring discussion of necessary sacrifice. They can review exciting, yet exceedingly unrealistic, opportunities for growth. They can make extraordinary, yet impractical, promises.

Many children are more than happy to be seduced into the business. And this can be for a number of reasons: the promise of wealth, power, freedom, status, or greatness.

Unfortunately, seduction relies on emotion, not rational thought. And when one is seduced into the family business (or seduced to stay), it is likely that one gives little thought to other options—this possibility becomes the only choice. It can become so enticing that one never gives any consideration whatsoever to pursuing a different path than the family business (perhaps one that would offer the same, or greater, achievements and rewards).

☑ SEDUCTION

"Being in the business meant being part of something important, and at the time I wasn't really feeling too important."

"I *think* my father is going to leave the business to me. At least that's what he said when I started—and that's the main reason I decided to work here."

"My mother told me that I was too good to work at a sandwich shop and that I should come work at the family business and be somebody."

"My parents told me I was next in line to own the business. But my parents are in their late seventies now, and I'm still waiting."

☑ FEAR

*"I don't know what else I could do, really.
This is all I've ever done."*

Fear can include fear of the unknown, fear of failing, fear of conflict or tension, or fear of disappointing others.

This cause is based on an inability to consider other job opportunities because these upsetting and negative emotions want to be avoided at all costs.

Sometimes the fear is based on reality, yet many times it is pure fantasy—nothing more than an idea of what *might* happen (or not happen) that has been built up over many years and has never been tested or challenged by anyone.

The fear develops a life of its own and can be self-defeating by blocking every attempt to even mull over another career path.

☑ **FEAR**

"How can I figure out what I really want to do with my life and, at the same time, deal with my family being mad at me? That's too much to deal with."

"I don't want to upset my (father/mother/ sibling/cousin)."

"I wouldn't know what to do if my parents were angry or really disappointed with me."

"I can't really point to any one thing and say I am *proud* of that, because I was never given anything that difficult to do. I don't think I could handle a real job."

☑ BY ACCIDENT

"It just kind of happened. I'm not sure how."

While it is unlikely that this would be the only reason to keep someone in a trapped family business situation, it is *exceedingly* common for children of family business owners to be working in the business without having had a plan or aspirations to do so.

Other reasons reinforce why someone stays trapped, but the first step, the entrance into the family business, may have happened without any actual planning or effort.

☑ BY ACCIDENT

"Mom and Dad went on vacation, and I stepped in full time and never left."

"It started as a part-time thing while I was looking for work after college, and then they needed more help, so I expanded my hours, and the next thing I knew, the job turned full time, and here I am fifteen years later."

☑ NO OTHER INTERESTS

*"I'm like my dad in that way. I think we both
ended up in the family business mostly because
we didn't really have anything else we cared
about—so why not this?"*

Some view work and career as an adventure to be
lived fully and passionately.

For others, work is simply a way to earn an income; for them, their "real lives" happen outside of
the hours of nine to five, and those who see work as
a calling or passion might puzzle them.

Being trapped may be the result of not possessing an interest or curiosity that leads directly to a
clear career path. It could also be the result of not
yet *finding* that interest or *discovering* that curiosity.

Without clear interests, or the ability, motivation,
or support to find them, staying in the family business becomes merely an adequate solution for a critical question: what do you really want to do?

☑ NO OTHER INTERESTS

"I've never really thought about my own career."

"I'm not sure what else I would do."

"I've never really thought this is what I am *supposed* to do this with my life—but it's not like there is something else that I really want to do anyway."

☑ LACK OF JOB SKILLS

*"How can I apply for a job by saying, 'For the
past eighteen years I've done a little of
everything...oh, and by the way, I've never
actually had a job title.' "*

Perhaps a family business, or a specific job, is so specialized and unique (or at least *seems* that way) that it's difficult to imagine how the skills to do that job would apply anywhere else.

Perhaps schooling was cut short, and not having a degree appears to be an insurmountable obstacle.

Unfortunately, for some, a lack of job skills and education can be real and is an actual roadblock to employment outside of the family.

Without looking into it, however, it is difficult to know if this is a real deficit or simply an imagined one. If skill development is needed, keep in mind that skills are not hard-wired talents, but behaviors that one acquires with training, education, and experience. Degrees are not given just to twenty-one-year-olds. Many universities have schools for professional or continuing education regardless of prior education, degrees, or age.

☑ LACK OF JOB SKILLS

"I hadn't really developed skills that would transfer to another business."

"That was all I could really do at the time."

"I knew how our business worked and could fill in for almost anyone, but not enough to really *do* their job."

"To do what I wanted, I would need a bachelor's degree, and I left college early to work in the business when my father died."

☑ "ROLE" IN THE FAMILY

*"My brothers were always fighting when we
were kids. I was the one who always had to
break things up. And I still have to. I'm
convinced this business would die a quick,
violent death if I wasn't here to step in."*

Put simply, the requirements of one's role in the
family can easily carry over to how work gets done
in the business.

Family therapists are typically trained to help
families see that we often play very distinct roles in
the "system" of a family. Examples include the care-
giver, the protector, the peacemaker, the troubled
kid, the winner, and the rescuer.

And in family businesses, unless these long-
standing (and often unconscious) family roles are
understood, they can be extremely limiting for the
individual as well as the business.

While a role may have served (and may still
serve) an important purpose in the family, or in a
family business, continuing to live out a role can

significantly restrain one's professional fulfillment as well as the success of the business.

☑ "ROLE" IN THE FAMILY

"I'm the one who watched my brothers and sisters when my parents weren't around—so of course I knew I would be the one in charge of the business when my parents wanted to retire."

"Growing up, Mom drank a lot; Dad was at work, (so) I took care of everything at home. When the kids were older, it was time for me to take care of work. My brother went off and did his own thing while I took care of the business and eventually took it over."

DARLA: PROMISES, PROMISES

Darla had grown up living in a house next door to the family business. The family generally spent nights, weekends, and holidays moving back and forth between home and their warehouse next door, where her father and mother's craft supply company was based.

The youngest of four siblings, Darla was named as her father's successor as a young teen, when she was the first to express an interest, though slight, in running the business someday. She spent her summers at home and in the warehouse. When it came time for college, her dad talked her into staying. He made the convincing argument that he would soon retire to start another enterprise and leave her to run this business and do what she wanted with it.

Years passed; Darla was still living with her parents in the house she grew up in, and she had stagnated professionally. She felt she had learned all she could about the business, had been successful in sales and operations, and was ready to take over—but Darla didn't want to push the issue.

Since her parents' divorce, she knew her dad relied on having her around. She didn't want her father to think he wasn't wanted or needed, and she knew that his heart and soul were in the business.

Her frustration increased, her siblings had all moved away, and Darla had somehow, without realizing it, filled the gap her mother left after the divorce… and she had no career plans, no ability to go out on her own, and very little satisfaction.

CHAPTER III

IDENTIFICATION:
WHAT DOES IT LOOK LIKE?

During my research for this book, I was surprised to encounter so many immediate reactions to the title. People seemed to "get it" instantly.

This concept of being trapped in the family business brought out stories and examples of people who felt this *emotionally*. Interestingly, very few mentioned anything about being *financially* trapped, despite the massive downturn in the global economy. Perhaps this was due to their awareness of my own psychology background and training—but what seems far more likely is that finances appear to be clear and measurable and can be dealt with using rational thought ("left-brain" thinking). For most, emotions are far more murky and complicated. Add to that the emotional complexity of families, and it becomes clear how so many become trapped.

Being emotionally trapped in a family business is not easy to discuss, and so it is often hidden, yet right below the surface. This becomes obvious when just mentioning the topic leads to an outpouring of stories.

The majority of adults were raised without the benefit of emotional or social skills training or education in school. Thankfully, many primary and secondary schools are now including curricula that help children and young adults understand and deal with a range of in*tra*- and in*ter*personal areas—conflict, assertiveness, empathy, and many others.

As a result, we are often not that well equipped to look at emotionally complicated issues, break them down into their most basic parts, consider a range of potential actions, and then implement a solution.

For too many of us, situations that center on relationships, personal identity, values, and other "soft" areas feel far too convoluted, too overwhelming, and too confusing.

So, these issues are dealt with by sidestepping the topic completely (avoidance), pretending they don't even exist (denial), or telling ourselves that there can't possibly be a reasonable solution (rationalizing). We convince ourselves that we should not "waste time" thinking or talking about them.

Because the field of psychological and behavioral research is not new, we have data (more than fifty years' worth) to help us understand what happens when we don't deal with emotionally complex situations.

Consider the following pages as only a sampling, a limited overview of a few of the consequences of avoided or unaddressed situations that are particularly relevant to family business settings. For each of those listed, there are variations, overlapping symptoms, and even potential medical diagnoses. So, remember: an accurate diagnosis should not and cannot be effectively made without consulting a licensed professional (see *Psychologists*, page 114).

Keep in mind that these problems (and their symptoms) can also be caused by a variety of conditions or circumstances that have nothing to do with a family business—including physical and/or other emotional roots. So, while they are not unique to being trapped in a family business, they might be indicators:

1. Substance Abuse

2. Depression

3. Work/Life Balance Problems

4. Lack of Engagement

5. Anxiety

6. No Challenges or Development

7. Little (or No) Satisfaction

8. Decreasing Influence and Power

1. SUBSTANCE USE AND ABUSE

Addiction is an increasingly common topic in family business books, at conferences, and among those who advise family businesses. There are now clinics around the country that specialize in addiction within family businesses.

Addiction can often be recognized at work by a pattern of any of the following: sudden and significant mood swings, falling asleep at a desk, coming in late, missed days, scattered thoughts, repeated lying, defensiveness, smelling like alcohol (an obvious but often overlooked indicator), as well as a host of others.

At the core of addiction is often a need to escape reality. The individual's situation may be overflowing with painful and disturbing feelings. Someone feels lost, angry, frustrated, depressed, or anxious—all of these are reasons why one may use substances to escape the everyday or numb oneself to it.

This type of escapism can be brought on, and maintained by, resentment toward parents, the business, or even oneself. And with more causes often comes more use—or abuse. This can include a need to use just to get through normal activities each day (addiction), so much so that increasing amounts of the substance are needed to have the same effect (known as "tolerance"). It can also result in painful withdrawal symptoms if the substance use is stopped (dependence). Withdrawal symptoms can include insomnia, nausea, tremors, seizures—and the list goes on.

Drinking or using drugs provides short-term relief (and release) but typically makes the overall situation worse and more difficult to deal with, especially when the substance wears off and nothing has changed in the situation that led to use in the first place. This is the heartbreaking cycle of substance abuse.

And as many of us know too well, the dark side of addiction includes increased inability to take care of oneself physically, emotionally, and socially. This can result in significant medical problems that end in disability or worse. Thus, perhaps, unconsciously, and sadly, addiction provides the ultimate and final escape from the family business—death.

2. DEPRESSION

When thinking about depression, it is critical to distinguish between everyday sadness and depression. Being alive means experiencing sadness from time to time. After all, life has disappointments, and all human beings must face loss at some point, whether it's the loss of loved ones, of opportunities, or of time. But, for most people, these moments or periods of sadness are not debilitating. They have effective, and various, ways of addressing it, coping with it, and moving on.

For those experiencing ongoing depressive symptoms, some of the common signs that can be seen for a period of weeks or months are:

- Depressed mood most of the day (on more days than not);
- Eating extremes (not wanting to eat at all or eating too much);
- Sleep problems (inability to fall asleep or stay asleep, or the opposite: needing much more sleep than usual);
- Inability to make decisions or concentrate;

- Feelings of hopelessness, pessimism, and lack of interest in the future;
- Low energy or fatigue so that work hours are shortened, and/or avoidance of any exercise or physical activity

While depression has received an impressive amount of coverage (books, movies, National Depression Awareness Day), there is a belief in the professional mental health community that a significant percentage of depression in the general population still goes undiagnosed and untreated. Sadly, this is, in part, due to the unfortunate and outdated belief that suffering from an emotional or psychological issue or illness implies personal failure or inadequacy.

3. WORK/LIFE BALANCE PROBLEMS

What can start as a strong work ethic or passion for the business can often result in having a life that revolves around work and only work. And, not surprisingly, research has confirmed this: the healthiest and happiest people have an overall balance between work, family, friends, and other interests.

Because working in a family business can blur the line between work and family (e.g., holidays are spent discussing business issues, and family arguments are acted out at work), being able to assess balance or imbalance is challenging at best, impossible at worst.

When asked about hobbies, friends, or just relaxing, some will say they have "no time," but what they are really saying is, "Those things are not as important as work." And, very typically, vacations are rare. Even if there is time away from the business, family members are usually "on call" in one way or another, and so they are unable to genuinely disengage from work. This lack of balance, over time, can negatively affect one's mental and physical health.

4. LACK OF ENGAGEMENT

When researchers looked at differences between individuals who had been in life-or-death situations and those who had not, they found that those who had come close to dying had a greater sense of meaning and purpose than the others. This can be explained in two ways.

For some, the proximity of death had given them a desire to live life more fully, due to their increased understanding of how fragile and short life is. For others, research supports that their ability to survive in a life and death situation might have been increased by their own intrinsic sense of meaning and purpose.

Although it's fictional, you can see this phenomenon play out in the film *It's a Beautiful Life*. A father imprisoned in a Nazi concentration camp shields his son from the torture and death around them by pretending that they are playing an elaborate game instead of being jailed in a death camp. In the film, the father's spirit and vitality are maintained while the other prisoners have seemingly lost hope and purpose.

To connect this to family business work, individuals who find themselves disengaged from their work and lacking a sense of meaning or purpose are far more likely to feel trapped than those who are fully engaged in it. They might feel numb, have no real interest in achieving their work goals, or be completely indifferent to trying something new or innovative.

If you are "phoning it in" and not actively doing something about it, you are trapped. And if you are in a leadership position, though not intended, this lack of personal engagement can affect employee morale and output and be a terribly destructive influence on the business.

5. ANXIETY

Similar to other topics in this chapter, it is important to distinguish between everyday worry and a diagnosable anxiety disorder. It is typical to worry about any number of things in life—health, children, and finances, to name a few. But when these worries become never ending and interfere with daily living, a professional consultation is warranted. There are many ways that anxiety can show itself, and many overlap with depression. These include:

- Constant, excessive worry (on more days than not)
- Restlessness
- Fatigue
- Irritability
- Sleep disturbances (difficulty falling or staying asleep)
- Muscle tension or pain
- Chronic health problems (often related to digestion)

6. NO CHALLENGES OR DEVELOPMENT

Human beings are wired for lifelong learning, whether it is becoming better at our jobs, learning how to manage relationships better, or adapting because of major life events, such as getting married or having children.

In any of these situations, we have to stretch ourselves, learn new skills, and embrace different mindsets. Without this, for most people life can quickly become tedious, pointless, and empty.

Many companies understand this, and while it may not contribute directly to the bottom line, they create and implement professional development plans for every employee—plans that may include new projects, cross training, workshops, coaching, job rotation—almost anything that will take an employee out of his or her usual routine.

In family businesses, there is often no single person charged with the responsibility of creating or supporting development plans for employees and managers—and sometimes no one to even champion the fact that ongoing development is necessary.

The focus is staying on top of operational tasks, sales goals, or other business needs—not individual employee needs.

Unfortunately, this often results in ignoring a basic need of the trapped person: to learn, grow, and develop.

7. LITTLE (OR NO) SATISFACTION

A common topic researched by organizational psychologists is what makes people happy at work and what makes them miserable. These two distinct factors are known as *satisfiers* and *dissatisfiers*. The lack of the first and/or too many of the second can cause problems, including frequent employee and management turnover.

Now, while both satisfiers and dissatisfiers can exist in any business, it can be more challenging to identify a lack of satisfiers in a family business. In part, this is because gauging individual fulfillment typically requires some reflection, while annoyances will always make themselves known. And family businesses can be especially guilty of failing to consider, and give priority to, individual fulfillment.

Of course, there is not one path to satisfaction at work. For each individual, there can be multiple satisfiers, including reaching sales or operational goals, developing new products, deepening relationships, and creating and moving toward a long-term vision.

Given the many potential sources of work satisfaction, if time spent in the business feels pointless, meaningless, or monotonous, there is a problem.

8. DECREASING INFLUENCE (OR POWER)

This sign of being trapped in a family business can be subtle and easy to miss—at first. Perhaps there are slower responses to voice mails or e-mails—or no responses at all. Or maybe there is a growing pattern of being left out of key meetings "by accident." Or possibly, there is a rising feeling that people are just tolerating you instead of appreciating you, getting your input, or utilizing your expertise.

Decreasing influence at work could be due to numerous causes: for example, being promoted beyond one's actual capabilities; a change in the organizational structure; or, sadly, someone with more authority having implicitly or explicitly told employees not to work with you or follow your instructions.

Whatever the behaviors and the reasons behind them, the ability to get things done; to manage people or projects; or to steer a department, division, or organization might seem to be heading in the wrong direction. Above all else, this may be the strongest sign that something is going on. Whether others have "done" it consciously, or whether it's because of one's own behavior (or some combination of the two), it's critical to take a step back and determine if this is a trapped situation.

WHO DECIDES?

Being trapped can be felt only from the inside, no matter how the situation appears to others. Observations of someone else's work life can be remarkably different from that person's internal experience—even if two people are in the same family and have known each other since birth.

Being trapped in a family business is not a determination made by a committee. The input of others is critical, but a spouse, parent, cousin, therapist, or advisor does not make the final judgment. Therefore, the warning signs listed previously in this chapter are not going to have the same relevance to everyone.

In addition, there are those who have adjusted to being trapped—they don't seem to be in significant emotional pain (or exhibit any of these "symptoms") despite feeling that they are unable to change their situation. They may still feel that life could be better, that they have much more potential personally and professionally, but are not in a position to do anything about it.

If being trapped can result from a lack of focus on individual needs and feelings, it seems problematic (and ironic) if someone else makes this decision as well.

JOHN: WE ARE FAMILY

John was the older of two siblings and was raised by a largely absent mother and an alcoholic father. From a very young age, John took care of his little sister and, essentially, ran the household. He made sure that food was available, that he and his sister were clothed, that the house was kept in order, and that nobody really knew that his father was barely functional.

John's mother could not be bothered while she was working in the family business that her grandfather had started. His father repeatedly reminded him of that fact. He also knew his mother would react harshly if he asked for help. She was a "self-made" success and had a difficult time acknowledging anyone's struggles or difficulties. As time went on, John continued to run the house and care for his sister. He had become a "parentified child."

When the time came, John decided his only option was to attend college locally and continue to live at home. His mother told him she would pay for his education on the condition that he would major in business and come right into the family business upon graduation. John did just that, rotating through many areas of the business during his twenties.

His father died when John was twenty-eight, and his mother, feeling liberated, decided to spend more and more of her time in a warmer climate. Soon after, she turned the business over to John for day-to-day operations.

Although the opportunity seemed great from the outside, John did not feel ready to run the business. He still saw most employees as "aunts" and "uncles," he didn't fully understand large parts of the business, and he just didn't feel right about becoming a manager at this point.

John was making the best of this new situation, working long hours and weekends to get up to speed as quickly as possible. His social life suffered (not that he ever had one), and he remained single despite a strong desire to find someone, settle down, and have children.

CHAPTER IV

EXPLORATION:
WHAT SHOULD BE
CONSIDERED?

It can be a huge relief to realize that other people share your experiences and are trapped in their family business as well—that your situation is not as unique as you may think. I have witnessed this repeatedly in my work with clients, as well as in the interviews I completed for this book.

These insights by themselves may be enough for some. However, for others they are only a first step. Next comes the work of looking inward, involving others, and making the best possible decision with this changed perspective. There is also the challenge, for some, of acting cautiously rather than impulsively, productively rather than destructively.

This chapter is for those who are ready and interested in better understanding their current predicament in their family business, including what is most important to them, as well as those who are ready to take action.

These steps are divided into the following sections:

A. Key Considerations

B. Important People

A. KEY CONSIDERATIONS

Regardless of how or why it happened, if you are reading this book because you may be trapped, you probably realize that you want something to change.

As part of your process for determining the next steps that you may want to take, start by taking a step back—or four steps, to be exact.

Considering the following four areas on the pages that follow will help you gain additional clarity and move you forward in your thinking. While some prefer to consider these factors through self-reflection, others may want to include friends, family, advisors, or other professionals in this exploration.

✦ HISTORY

✦ LEGACY

✦ RELATIONSHIPS

✦ CAREER

✦ HISTORY

*Those who cannot remember the
past are condemned to repeat it.*

— George Santayana,
The Life of Reason

Whether it's because of sibling relationships, family dynamics, or work culture, most professionals who work with family businesses will tell you that it is absolutely critical to understand the history of the family business: how it developed, who achieved what, and what key decisions were made, to name a few.

However, the desire to understand and appreciate the *family business* history is very different from the need to understand *personal* history in the family business. In other words, what is your own story of joining the business? Did it start when you were a child? Was it your request or your parents' request? When did the business become your full-time career? Have you ever left the family business? Why did you leave? Why did you return? What was your first job in the business?

I have been surprised at how many of my clients cannot easily remember those details. At first, I hear, "I don't remember exactly," or, "I think I was born here."

✦ LEGACY

"Everyone must leave something behind when they die…It doesn't matter what you do, so long as you change something from the way it was before *you touched it into something that's like you after you take your hands away."*

— Ray Bradbury,
Fahrenheit 451

Everyone rates his or her own personal legacy across a broad spectrum of importance, from "Legacy doesn't really enter my mind" all the way to "There is nothing more important than what I leave behind." Considering your own legacy, regardless of your age, is critical when you are considering changing something about your relationship with the family business.

Rate this a scale of 1-10, where 1 signifies little interest and 10 symbolizes an intense commitment to leaving a strong legacy for the next generation(s).

Depending on your own feelings, experiences, and personality, contributing to the ongoing legacy of the family business and what this business has become may provide intense satisfaction for you, or it may have no impact on you whatsoever.

What about the ability to introduce your children to the family business? Do you believe that it might someday be important to be able to connect your children to it?

Do you want to have an impact on what the family business looks like in ten years…or twenty years…or fifty years? Or perhaps you doubt you can, or will, have an impact?

The answers to these questions will help shine a light on the value of remaining in, shaping, or leaving the family business.

✦ RELATIONSHIPS

"A relationship, I think, is like a shark, you know? It has to constantly move forward or it dies. And I think what we got on our hands is a dead shark."

— Woody Allen & Marshall Brickman,
Annie Hall

Spending time thinking about key relationships is the third consideration and, for some, the most important.

With family and work being intertwined in a family business, it can become very confusing and difficult to sort through which relationships are the most important. It will take effort, but it is important to clarify who matters to you most; who influences you the most; whom you trust; whom you admire. Zeroing in on these people will make it easier for you to better understand your situation, what you may want to change, and what you may want to keep the same.

Although we sometimes may fool ourselves into thinking we can, and should be able to, function fully independently, in reality not much happens in this world without other people. Some would argue that *nothing* happens in isolation.

So take some time to reflect on this. Consider who will be affected by any changes you make and how important that is to you. Try not to focus on the "right" way to think. Do not worry about what these answers say about you—simply try to answer honestly without censoring yourself.

You may not consider a parent someone who is central to your life. You may have a relationship with a nonfamily business colleague that is more important to you than any family relationship. Try to be brutally honest with yourself as to who really matters at this point in your life. This will guide which relationships you put the most effort into and which you do not.

✦ CAREER

Father: One day, lad, all this will be yours! (pointing out the window)

Son: What, the curtains?

Father: No, not the curtains, lad. All that you can see! Stretched out over the hills and valleys of this land! This'll be your kingdom, lad!

Son: But Father, I don't want any of that. I'd rather...just...sing!

— from the film
*Monty Python and
the Holy Grail*

For many who are trapped in the family business, choosing one's own career path was never really an option. It may be challenging to appreciate, but even if you never chose your work or held a formal title, as long as you have worked somewhere, you have developed skills.

Many of my clients think they are unable to do anything else professionally, only to find, with a little digging, that the skills they picked up in the family business are actually very transferable to other businesses in other industries or even in other parts of the world.

So, career reflection should include questions such as:

- If I could do anything, what would I do for a career?
- Is there an interest or path that I forgot about or abandoned? What was it, and why did I lose sight of it?
- What do I like about what I am doing now?
- What don't I like?
- Could I build a better, or even an ideal, career somewhere in this family business?

As I mentioned in the beginning of chapter 2, an "arranged career" often exists in family businesses. And, like an arranged marriage, that career is often not in the best interest of the child but rather the family, often without anyone realizing it.

Even if you decide to make no changes whatsoever to your situation, everyone is entitled to at least consider, or dream about, what type of work would provide the greatest satisfaction. Just the act of trying to answer the question may provide clarity and direction.

B. IMPORTANT PEOPLE

Ultimately you will make your own decisions, but you should probably not make decisions simply from reading a book. For some of you, this is an obvious point. For those who aren't thinking of involving others in the decision, consider this:

Have you ever sought input on these decisions?

- What college to attend and/or major to choose
- Which car to buy
- Where to go on vacation
- What wine to choose
- What clothes to wear

To further emphasize this point, if you involve others in these types of decisions, wouldn't you involve people in your decision about what to do about your next step with the family business?

Now the question turns to *whom* to talk with. Some people who immediately may come to mind are friends, siblings, cousins, parents, business advisors, religious or spiritual leaders, therapists, and teachers.

Regardless of whom you decide to involve, you should make sure that you connect with at least one person who has *no stake* in your actions or decisions. The people who will be affected the most by what you do are the *least* able to be objective and consider your best interests above all else—whether we realize it or not, it is virtually impossible to be neutral when we will be directly involved in an outcome of a decision. People involved in the family business might have a very difficult time separating their *own* needs from what is best for *you*.

Would you ask a Mercedes dealer (and no one else) to list the reasons why you should buy a Mercedes? Likewise, would you only ask a BMW dealer for the list of reasons *not* to buy a Mercedes? Both have interests in the outcome of your decision, as does any family business member when you are considering changing your involvement or role in the family business.

The conflict of interest here is obvious (your needs versus the salesperson's). In fact, in professions such as medicine and psychology, it is considered unethical to treat your family because it is widely believed that there is an inherent and unavoidable lack of objectivity when treating a family member.

Involving true outsiders might also result in the discussion of items that might have gone ignored otherwise:

- Long-term financial impact
- Ongoing interactions with extended family members (e.g., family gatherings, weddings, etc.)
- Opportunities for children

An external colleague or independent advisor who does not work for the family business is more at liberty to ask the hard questions because he or she is less likely to have an investment in the final decision.

If you have been surrounded by the family business your entire life, this may be harder to grasp because your network of colleagues, friends, and advisors are all involved in the business in one way or another.

So, for some, this may mean developing a new relationship completely outside of the business and your family, such as hiring an objective professional or becoming involved in a group advisory board or roundtable.

The next section provides an overview of the value of these resources and explains how to find them.

✦ FINDING OTHERS JUST LIKE YOU

If there is only one thing you take from this book, it should be this: your experience of suppressing your own ambitions or goals for the good of the family and/or family business is not unique.

Having met, interviewed, and worked with many of these individuals (people who are trapped are surprisingly easy to find, once you start asking), I know that many of you are living (and working) in isolation. You are unaware that others feel this way, and you haven't had the opportunity to find or connect with them.

One of the most helpful things you can do for yourself is to find others in the same or similar situations. Why is this helpful? Because just about all human beings feel shame or embarrassment *when they believe their situation (or feeling, or experience) is strange or unusual*. And that shame or embarrassment gets in the way of solving problems and improving situations.

In a family business, it can be especially tricky, because you likely do not, and cannot, share your personal thoughts with coworkers. By contrast, in nonfamily business settings, coworkers can be a great source of support and feedback. At the very least, they can be a bit more objective than a sibling or parent.

When you are able to realize and see that others are in the same boat as you, it increases your own ability to be thoughtful and honest. Most importantly, it saves time and energy that would be wasted on blaming yourself for not being like everyone else.

When you learn that others have experienced the same situations, feelings, and thoughts you have, it can be a great relief. You may find that you are suddenly liberated—to search for solutions, to speak with others more candidly, and to see your situation as just that—a *situation*, not a prison sentence, a terminal illness, or a fundamental flaw in your character.

You can find others like you in a number of different ways:

- Seek out a local *university-based family business center*. These organizations typically have monthly or quarterly meetings and workshops where you could find others in family businesses who might be helpful to you (see *Professional Resources*, page 113).

- Find like-minded people in other family businesses by asking a trusted advisor (accountant, attorney, financial advisor) if he or she could introduce you to other clients who may be questioning their role or future in their family business. You may be surprised at the number of individuals you find.

✦ TALKING TO ADVISORS

Trusted professional advisors can provide a wealth of support, information, and solutions. You may find that your financial advisor, attorney, accountant, or family office can not only introduce you to others in similar family business situations, but also help you sort through some of the complex issues you are facing.

After all, these individuals have relationships with others in your family business and might have recommendations for how you could approach them about your current state of affairs. Also, many advisors possess years of experience confronting similar family business issues and might have stories to share with you about what strategies work and which do not.

Of course, you may want to ask for complete confidentiality, just in case they are currently employed by the family business and are accountable to someone other than you. Some advisors may feel obligated (legally or otherwise) to share the content of your discussion(s), while others may not. Make sure you know these limits of confidentiality, if there are any.

✦ TALKING TO OTHER PROFESSIONALS

Psychologists and career counselors can assist you in ways that your business advisors cannot. As when selecting any specialist, you should consider his or her relevant training and experience, your own personal sense of comfort with, and trust in, this professional, as well as confidentiality limits (again). After all, you should find someone you can be completely honest and direct with, without fear of judgment or exposure.

By providing completely objective feedback (possibly including personality and values assessments or career testing), these specialists are in a unique position to assist you. While business advisors might earn their living selling financial products, creating legal documents, or filing taxes, these professionals typically charge for their time only.

Both psychologists and career counselors may be trained in, and focus on, the "system" of a family business. Some believe it is critical to involve other key family players in any family business consultation work they do. While this approach can be very helpful, it is important to consider whom in the family you want included in your work together, *if anyone*.

You may prefer to work with someone who specializes primarily in working with individuals rather than the whole family, although having a "systems" perspective is still important. Make sure to explore and discuss these two approaches (individual vs. system) and what it means for you as you research and meet with potential advisors (see pages 113-115).

✦ TALKING TO FAMILY

You may be comfortable right now having a frank and direct conversation with your parents or other family members about feeling trapped in the business. Or maybe not.

Regardless of where you currently stand on this, it is still helpful to consider what this type of conversation might be like, and the many directions it could go in.

Being direct and honest can be an effective strategy, but given the complex dynamics in family businesses, it could also create all sorts of questions that you are not ready to answer—or have no idea how to answer. It might also create tension and conflict that you are not prepared for or may want to avoid.

You would need to be very clear about what you hope to accomplish through such a conversation and have an idea of how to start it and how to end it.

For example, do you simply want to communicate your dissatisfaction or frustration? Or maybe you want to get some advice.

Perhaps you know how to start the discussion (e.g., "There is something I really want to talk about that I've been thinking about for quite awhile. And I'm coming to you because I think you can help, and I need your help"), but no idea about how to end it (e.g., "I think I've gone as far as I can go with this right now, and I need some time to think about what you have said. Can we talk about this again soon?").

A little effort and planning now can help you feel more in control of the conversation, especially if the conversation is with a parent. Considering and planning this conversation could be done with assistance from that trusted advisor, friend, counselor, or colleague.

DEBBIE: TAKE A LOOK AT ME NOW

Debbie and her brother, John, had worked in the family business since they were teenagers. Her father's retail chain was a tremendous success, and both Debbie and John continued to work there during breaks from college.

After four years of working full time in various parts of the business, John left to follow his dream of a career in engineering. Debbie did not have clear career interests, so she stayed. Though she had been able to work successfully with her father during her eight years in the business, Debbie yearned for complete control.

One spring day, her father asked her into his office to meet three people who had agreed to buy the business. Debbie was completely caught off guard. She and her father had never discussed his retirement, but she thought at the very least that her father would explore the possibility of a family purchase or partial gifting of the business.

Debbie felt horrible. She believed that her father ultimately did not have faith in her and that he didn't think she could run the business. Debbie had spent much of her childhood trying to get her father's attention, as he was most often tied up with the business and her brother's athletics. She thought this sudden sale was another example of her father's ignoring her and her capabilities.

A friend suggested that, if she was serious, she should approach her father directly about buying the business. Debbie thought this would show her father she was serious and could actually be a success.

So she found a business consultant, put a plan together, and approached her father. It took convincing, but after they worked out key issues, her father was sold. Debbie had gotten just what she wanted.

Unfortunately, while Debbie and her consultant had done a great job creating a business plan, she failed to ask herself if this was what she truly wanted or if other factors were at play.

After just eighteen months, Debbie lost her spirit and energy and realized that she had pursued this venture primarily because of her need to prove herself to her father, not because she wanted to be a small-business owner.

CHAPTER V

ACTION:

WHAT CAN BE DONE?

There are many creative and effective options available to someone trapped in the family business. Of course, some are easier to execute than others, and each situation deserves its own analysis and plan. The goal of this section is *not* to provide a systematic guide for what to do for every situation.

Rather, it is to create a very broad set of options to consider what might be possible.

Another result of being trapped in the family business is that options for changing your situation can seem alternately overwhelming or pointless. Certainly, any action that targets such a potentially complicated scenario will have advantages and disadvantages, and so each should be considered carefully.

For ease of organization, I have divided these into three broad categories:

1. Change perspective.

2. Take action.

3. Exit.

1. CHANGE PERSPECTIVE

After considering the questions in the last chapter, or having a heart-to-heart with a family member, or perhaps speaking to an advisor, you may decide that no action is needed.

Through self-reflection or talking, some people are able to significantly change their understanding of their role, or what the family business means to them, or have a more specific plan for the future, so that their sense of being trapped dissipates.

This shift to a more positive, less trapped perspective sometimes happens easily because many of one's feelings about the family business can be based on faulty assumptions (e.g. they expect me to stay here forever; my contributions aren't appreciated; if I tell them I'm unhappy, they won't care). And unless addressed directly, these issues can build over time and seem much larger than they actually are.

It is quite possible that conversations, thoughtful introspection, or simply hearing that others support you is enough to extinguish your trapped condition. An open expression of frustration, disappointment, and conflict coupled with an ability to listen is sometimes all that is needed to fundamentally shift one's mind-set.

If the actions you have taken until this point have not resulted in this type of change, it might be time to consider option #2.

2. TAKE ACTION

Each of the following actions involves staying in the family business and finding a way to shift what you do on a daily basis so that you are more satisfied and effective, happier, and less trapped. They may or may not be possible based on your current role, timing, the business you are in, or others' reactions to these options.

◆ Modify the job.

◆ Switch your role.

◆ Change the business.

✦ MODIFY THE JOB

There may be a significant component of your work that is a poor fit for your personality, your interests, or your abilities. You may also be getting bored in your role, having been in it for many years. Again, it is important to remember that many family businesses can be particularly inadequate when it comes to creating and documenting job responsibilities and development paths for family members.

If this is the case, and you haven't already considered it, you may be able to alter your role enough to provide variety, challenge, stimulation, or something else that you are currently missing (i.e., a key *satisfier*). For example, find a project that is a bit outside your everyday activities. More specifically, if you are based primarily in operations, explore being part of a marketing project, or if you are in sales, consider taking on the role of training a junior employee.

A change in job title is not needed to accomplish any of these goals. However, involving others *is* usually necessary.

First, map out those parts of your role that you would be pleased to let go of (without censoring yourself, no matter how unrealistic your hopes may be), as well as the things you would like to add or expand. This is only a first step, but it also may be all you need to significantly change how you feel about being in the family business.

For more help with this process, you may want to seek out an experienced career counselor (see page 113).

✦ SWITCH YOUR ROLE

While this may be more complicated and could potentially entail other family members changing their roles, it may also be a relatively easy solution to your situation. If you have not spent time in other roles in the company, consider moving around. This may be especially helpful if you have worked only in the family business.

While it may not be a typical move for family members, spending time in a less influential position in the company could be enlightening and provide you with perspectives you would not gain otherwise.

Have you ever worked on the manufacturing floor as an individual contributor (not managing others)? Or in the office as a generalist? The financial implications of this would need to be addressed, as well as the nature of the assignment (e.g., is this part of a larger rotation? Would this be until further notice or for a specific period of time?). It may be helpful to also consider any potential gaps in the company and how you may be able to help yourself and the company by creating and filling a brand-new role.

✦ CHANGE THE BUSINESS

Relative to the first two potential actions, this option would be the most substantial. If you are in a leadership role and can research this carefully while gaining support from others, significantly changing the business could provide a wonderful opportunity for you to enhance your effectiveness and satisfaction.

This type of change might range from becoming primarily a retail or distribution organization rather than a manufacturing one; or it could mean abandoning traditional markets in order to enter new ones; or it could mean specializing in one product or service rather than a broad range.

Typically reserved only for the owner or founder who does not want to sell or leave the business, this strategy is often employed multiple times during the lifespan of a business—sometimes to keep the owner or founder engaged and excited about his or her work or simply to keep up with changing times. The entrepreneurial spirit often craves this type of transformation and activity.

If you find yourself (and others) in agreement that the business is stagnating, that the industry is changing significantly, or that your satisfaction has been suffering, then recreating the business may be just what is needed.

Clearly, this change would require professional input and extensive research, and would be a major shift not just for you, but potentially for the company as a whole.

For those who are up to this particular challenge, the satisfaction of a successful transformation can far outweigh the risk and effort involved.

3. EXIT

What follows are the most significant decisions and the most drastic changes that someone can make in attempting to change their current situation.

These options often *feel* the best—and sometimes *are* the best. But it's important to take some time to determine whether doing something extreme is the best decision, a reasonable one, or an impulsive one.

Given the significance of each of these, you must take great care in considering, understanding, and planning your future. While you can't predict exactly what might happen after choosing one of these courses of action, you certainly can prepare for what will likely come—many adjustments, some with both positive and negative implications:

- In relationships
- In daily activities
- In finances
- In status
- In power
- In influence
- In identity

From work done with people in retirement, it is clear that the "dream" of life after work is frequently not at all what they thought it would be. More and more people end up desperate for activity, goals, and work. Some, sadly, sink into boredom, depression, or worse.

So consider, understand, and plan as best you can before opting for an extreme solution. You can make sure you do your homework and base your decision on a thorough examination of your options:

✦ Leave the business

✦ Sell the business

✦ LEAVE THE BUSINESS

When deciding whether or not to leave, you must address key issues such as changes in ownership status or percentage of ownership. This is not only for financial reasons, but also because both those leaving and those staying may have very different ideas about what type of continued impact or influence is appropriate or desired for the family member who is exiting.

And, considering that life is never certain, neither are family businesses. After time spent away, you may find that you want to return. Although that may be impossible to conceive at this point, you should consider how to leave so that you don't close too many doors on the way out. Perhaps framing your departure as a "leave of absence" is the best solution, with clear guidelines and time frames for returning unless something better happens. This is especially true if the only place you have ever worked is the family business. Do you really know what you will find? Can you be completely sure that anything else will be better than what you have now?

You may find that time away from the family business inspires an idea that could help the family transform the business in ways no one has imagined (e.g., a groundbreaking product, an innovative service, a new approach to sales). This possibility alone might be enough for you to contemplate the idea of being able to return someday.

And although emotions may be running high (or you are simply exhausted at this point), consider framing your departure in terms of your personal "fit" with the business or even "just seeing what else is out there."

Either of these is arguably a more reasonable and less abrasive explanation than blaming the business or going on record to say that you believe the business or its leadership is deeply flawed or dysfunctional.

Now that may absolutely be the case, but you need to remember your primary goals—do you want to satisfy an emotional need (the classic "you can take this job and...") while burning bridges, or do you want to find a strategy that benefits you, both in the short and long term? Perhaps you feel that the family and the business will benefit from hearing this, and that you owe it to them, but what price will this cost you personally? Sometimes the messenger does get shot.

The more you can "own" your decision to leave, the greater the likelihood of feeling in control of your departure and of not being victimized by the situation and business.

This should be a decision you've made because you have considered your options, weighed them carefully, and put yourself first. If it feels more like a quick getaway (or a jailbreak), then you may not have done all your homework yet.

If you decide to leave, something else to keep in mind is *when* you want to depart. Do you want to give enough notice so that the company, if necessary, can find and get a replacement up and running in your role? Or perhaps that isn't necessary, but you still want time to finalize your plans for what you will do after leaving. Or maybe you have your plan (e.g., another job, starting your own business, taking time off) and you are ready to go—but you first decide to think carefully about some of the earlier questions in this book. For example, which relationships (for business or family or other personal reasons) do you want to keep intact? And how can you leave while at the same time nourishing those relationships? Will extra time help?

The bottom line is: if you leave, do so with eyes wide open—with the knowledge that, while this may be your best possible decision for right now, change inevitably involves losses as well as gains.

✦ SELL THE BUSINESS

You may be in the fortunate position of being the sole owner of the family business, and you can make the decision to sell without needing others to buy in.

However, given that this is a family business, even if other family members don't have an ownership stake, they likely depend on the business in a number of ways—emotionally and financially, as well as for their sense of purpose and legacy.

Selling the business to siblings or other members of the family may be what you need—while also maintaining much of the opportunity for them and perhaps for your offspring (if structured this way), yet relieving you of the burden of day-to-day operations. Again, exploring what that means to you— and how important it is for you to protect or ignore those needs—will influence the sale.

Perhaps you will negotiate partial ownership and/or influence for your other family members. Or, maybe you will maintain a role on an advisory board so that you can still influence the strategy and future direction of the business (this is a tricky one, but it can be done successfully). Each of these potential adjunct roles should be created with the help of an experienced family business specialist.

Ultimately, selling the business removes you from the day-to-day running of it. You will be freeing yourself from the responsibility of creating the future vision of the business, as well as implementing strategies to get there.

Hopefully, if you go this route, you have explored all of your options and decided that this particular business is not the answer for your long-term happiness or satisfaction. Perhaps you have found something else you were *meant* to do at this point in your life.

Now, for many, a significant amount of cash to start a new business may be far more helpful than staying in the family business. Selling the business, I believe, is a last resort and, more than any other option, must be considered with the involvement and input of multiple other individuals, including family members, advisors, and experts.

MARK: A PERFECT STORM

Mark was the oldest of three children, with a father who had achieved tremendous success in business process management consulting. He had worked in the company one summer before college, and again between sophomore and junior years.

After graduating, Mark spent three more months at the firm before finding a job related to his major, banking. After four years, he was let go because of a downsizing. This left Mark without work or direction. He hadn't really enjoyed banking but also knew that he wasn't going to follow his passion in music because of the industry and its unpredictability. So he came back to his dad's firm while he figured out his next move.

For the first time, his father starting talking to him about becoming a permanent part of the company and offered to pay to send him to business school. Mark thought an MBA would be helpful regardless of his next step, and he also realized that his father needed a great deal of help.

Mark started learning all aspects of the business, from bookkeeping to marketing to sales and operations. He found that the firm's finances had been mismanaged, that employees and managers had taken advantage of him over many years, and that the business would likely close if his dad were to leave or die unexpectedly. So, Mark found himself working for considerably less money and longer hours than ever before—and working with a father who was not terribly motivating or appreciative.

Despite this, Mark's role gave him some confidence and a sense of purpose. However, even if he wanted to, Mark realized that he would not be able to leave until the business was much more stable and profitable, as his father was counting on selling the business for his retirement.

CHAPTER VI

BALANCE
WHAT MUST BE REMEMBERED?

One of the most widely used models for understanding the complexity of family-owned enterprises is the Tagiuri and Davis Three-Circle Model developed in the 1970s. If you have ever attended a family business workshop or read a family business book, you might have seen it. The model is brilliant in its simplicity. It depicts three overlapping circles which demonstrate that there are many potential identities for anyone involved in a family business: Are you an owner? Are you a family member? Do you work in the business? Some combination or two or more? This model clarified the need to understand multiple roles and perspectives when considering business structure, processes, and decision-making.

Since first publishing this book in 2012, I have identified the need for an additional circle to highlight another critical differentiator in family business work:

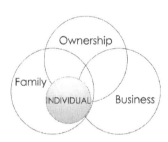

Including a fourth circle helps raise key questions that I have found are often overlooked:

1. How does the individual fit in the family? In what ways are they similar? In what ways are they different? Personality? Values? Experiences? Goals?

2. How does the individual choose to utilize their ownership or employment role? To what extent are these other identities important or central to their lives?

Ken Kaye, PhD, a retired psychologist from Chicago, identified the "kid brother" syndrome in family business because it was common to find a sibling who was not making valuable work contributions yet was tolerated and protected because of his familial status. In most cases, this sibling is a problem for everyone around, especially during times of succession or sale of the business. But also, being that kid brother came with a great internal cost; namely, to live as a burden rather than an actively contributing member of a business. For everyone to tolerate this situation often means that there is little interest in finding a better fit for him professionally elsewhere, and that perhaps he is not thought worthy or capable enough to explore other options in life. It is not overly dramatic to consider this a tragedy on many fronts.

So, by including this extra circle, by introducing a "Four-Circle Model," my hope is to force the issue of individual difference in the broader context of family, ownership, and employment.

As I continue to travel and speak about this topic, it has become clear that family business stories can shine a spotlight on what are normal human developmental experiences; In this case, that specific experience is the process of self-differentiation. Every human being has to be able to find the ways in which they can be different, disagree, and manage conflict with their family. While there are important cultural differences to this process, every person who makes it to adulthood must pass through this phase of lifespan development. For more on this topic, I encourage exploring the work of various leaders and writers in this field including Murray Bowen, Erik Erikson, and Daniel Levinson.

In family business, this task becomes more complex. It is far simpler and easier to "separate" and form a unique identity when one has a completely independent career or work-life. Moving away from a childhood town, going off to college, and finding one's own career path all serve this developmental process well. However, this normal part of growing up becomes much trickier, to quote the title of Greg McCann's book, "When your parents sign the paychecks."

I utilize the following two constructs to help my clients stay focused of the importance of that fourth circle, especially given the complexities of differentiation when growing up in a family business: self-actualization and family engagement.

A. Self-actualization:
to become everything one is capable of becoming.

While this term has various definitions and has been around in the academic and pop psychology literature for many years, it is especially important when family business is involved. Within the realm of work, striving towards self-actualization translates to keeping in mind, and exploring, the kind of roles, responsibilities, and activities that provide opportunities for you to build on who you are, and who you strive to be. Continually keeping an eye on this concept means that you will pull from your natural (and acquired) skills and resources to pursue the kind of things that make you feel most alive and consistent with your values and personality. What feels the most like you? When are you able to bring your full self to work? In what types of work situations do you find yourself most frequently in a state of flow (Csikszentmihalyi, 1990)?

B. Family engagement:
the potential to benefit from familial intimacy and interdependence

You can take a person out of their family (business), but you can't take the family out of the person. Even if you were to decide to leave your family business and never speak to another family member for the rest of your life, you will always share some genetics with family as well as be shaped by early experiences with them. Effective adult functioning includes the ability for you to determine your own interest in, and goals for, engagement with your family of origin. Keeping in mind the fourth circle above, every individual in a family is going to experience their desires, expectations, and perspectives for family engagement differently. However, a key component of striving towards a personal level of family engagement is the realization that families, and family businesses, can bring opportunities to be known and to know others in ways that will never be possible with other human beings who aren't in your family. Shared experiences and DNA aren't everything, but they cannot be replaced. It is critical though to keep in mind that family engagement is not simply time spent together, holiday meals, or shared vacations; More importantly, it is the willingness to keep sharing parts of ourselves (both the good parts as well as the uncomfortable ones) with family members as well as being open to seeing other sides of them that build intimacy.

Both of these are lifelong pursuits. Based on circumstances, life events, or unforeseen issues, one or both of these concepts might take a back seat to more pressing needs. However, when working in a family business, it becomes especially critical to remain conscious of both of these key parts of life since they can easily move out of balance. Time can move quickly, and before we know it, we have spent a lifetime doing work that we find hasn't moved us towards greater self-actualization and simultaneously, has blocked the development of family engagement as a fully functioning adult.

CHAPTER VII

PARENTING
HOW CAN THIS BE PREVENTED?

I rarely encounter parents who want to trap their children in a family business. More often than not, they begin to wonder if they have somehow accidentally contributed, or might contribute, to this type of situation with their child. Most simply want the family business to be an opportunity that could provide their children with freedom, success, and job options in a way that non-family employment could not. While this chapter won't address some of the potentially unconscious and self-serving needs of parents when it comes to employing their children, it will provide six fairly straightforward and generally accepted methods for avoiding a trapped dynamic.

1. UTILIZE REPUTABLE ASSESSMENT TOOLS TO MEASURE PERSONALITY AND MOTIVATIONS

One of the most powerful development exercises I have seen family businesses go through together is the analysis, and comparison of psychometric data that focuses on personality traits, emotional intelligence skills, personal values, and interests. A client once compared viewing these reports that measure "soft" areas much like receiving test results from a physician; it is far easier to make decisions about your life when you can look at data. While no assessment tool is ever 100%, they can help articulate individual differences that should factor into making important hiring and development decisions. In his case, personality and career testing showed in black and white that he was not only a poor fit for a management role, but that business success was not an important motivator. Rather than spend 10 more years frustrated and angry for being in a job that didn't fit, he worked with his brother to arrange a buy out that made them both happier and kept their relationship from completely disintegrating.

The younger you are, the easier it is to convince yourself that your potential is unlimited; that any job or career path is viable. And often, as a parent, the more motivated you are to see your child succeed in your family's business, the more likely you are to have blinders on when it comes to seeing potential gaps. And while psychometrics are just one method of assessing an individual's potential in a particular role, career, or industry, they are a relatively small investment that is easily administered and used.

2. REQUIRE OUTSIDE WORK EXPERIENCE

An attorney recently told me that it is a good thing more family businesses do not address conflict in its earliest stages. "If they did," he continued, "things would rarely get as messy as they do and family business attorneys would be out of business." I might cynically add that it's a good thing that so many children do not seek outside employment before joining their family business; if they did, there would be far fewer people interested in this book and my help.

Sadly, what I see over and over again is that families are more than happy to avoid the discomfort (and implied risk) of having the next gen work elsewhere before joining the family business. Unfortunately, without those outside experiences, I have found there often exists a seed of doubt.: "Could I survive elsewhere?" "Am I actually a competent, independent person capable of functioning in the world?" This type of suspicion is difficult to undo without actual life or work experience. Parents (and advisors) can point out all sorts of work success internally, but as long as there is no first-hand outside experience to back it up, there is often that festering self-doubt among those who went directly into the family enterprise after school or college.

This type of requirement is also important to the health of the business itself. I've had clients that have never written a resume, been on a job interview, or held an official title. They feel like frauds who are just working on borrowed time, which then leads to dread, panic, and risk aversion if there is any possibility of the family business failing. These individuals also don't have the ability to draw from outside experiences, non-family mentors, or business failures (and successes) that were acquired on someone else's dime, but could be utilized to help the family business make informed, effective decisions.

3. CONSIDER OPTIONS FOR NEW VENTURES (LIQUIDITY)

When parents share how important it is to provide their children with an opportunity that they did not have themselves, employment in a family business seems to be an obvious path. However, there is increasing support for another option for children of family enterprises: providing (well-structured) financial backing for new ventures. Parents can serve as investors, board members, and advisors while giving their children the opportunity to create their own path and build a business or role for themselves that might be a far better fit. This option is sometimes used as a way to explore new products and services that might someday be integrated back into the main business. It also allows children the chance to steer their own ship and perhaps figure out that they need to spend more time learning from others before they take the helm of a more significant venture. Allowing small opportunities for failure can have very powerful effects when it comes to personal and professional growth.

Because of the normal developmental need to create an identity separate or distinct from one's family, children in their twenties often keep bumping up against their parents' authority. In family businesses, without clearly identified roles and responsibilities, this conflict becomes frequent and toxic. Creating a separate entity or project where children have increased separation and independence from parental supervision can enhance motivation while simultaneously avoiding conflict that is often more related to normal adult development than to specific family/business issues.

4. CREATE WRITTEN JOB DESCRIPTIONS

I recently interviewed a 28-year-old operations manager for a family business who was impressive in many ways. While there were opportunities for her to come into the business as a full-time employee, she did not do so until two conditions were possible:

a. Her parents were willing and able to pay her a salary comparable to what she was earning on her own.

b. A written job description was created that included key responsibilities and tasks as well as skills most needed for a specific role.

Interestingly, ownership had only been discussed in terms of various options that her parents might consider when retirement approached, including selling to her, other employees, or an external buyer. This young professional understood that working in her parents' business could provide many advantages that aren't available elsewhere. However, she was also clearly focused on making the best possible decisions about her work. Given that psychologically healthy perspective, isn't it logical that she would want a clear job description? And, who among us would be comfortable with our children starting a job somewhere without one?

5. ENFORCE BARRIERS TO ENTRY

Making exceptions for family members is rarely a good decision. This is especially true when entering the business. Some of the most troubling exceptions I've witnessed are:

- Requiring 5+ years of outside employment, but accepting less than 2 because of "timing."
- Cobbling together random responsibilities in order to create a role for a family member because they need work, not because the business has a need.
- Placing a family member in a job despite a written requirement for a specific degree, experience, or knowledge that they do not possess.

Rules and processes about hiring employees (and specifically family members) are created and implemented effectively when rational decision-making processes are used, various factors are taken into account, and human resource/advisor expertise can be utilized. Exceptions to those rules and processes are more typically made when unconscious or emotional factors play a role. And when that happens, the trap is set.

6. ESTABLISH A FAMILY COUNCIL

Treating family members the same as non-family employees is not only an unrealistic position, but would also serve to destroy the advantages that family businesses can provide...and those advantages serve not only individuals, but also the business as a whole. We know that family-owned companies often make decisions based on long-term perspectives more than other businesses do. We also know that, when your name is on the door/building/product, the business has a history that dates back to your great grandparents, and you have seen the positive impact of your family business on the community/region/world, you are more likely to work harder and care more than someone who doesn't share those attributes.

Family councils and family meetings are structured processes for making sure that family values, transitions, events, unity, education, conflict, and professional development among other topics can be addressed directly. Many of them provide outlets for any family member to have a voice while also serving to maintain focus on the added complexities inherent to family enterprises.

These meetings are tools that can be used to provide early detection and intervention for family members who might be in a wrong job, or need additional support, or simply need to voice their own concerns, hopes, or lack of clarity related to their role and future in the business. Ideally organized and facilitated by an outsider, family councils and meetings can serve to ensure that uncomfortable issues find their way into the open rather than remain buried, only to surface with greater conflict and upheaval later.

IN CLOSING

*"If you choose not to decide, you
still have made a choice."*

— Neil Peart, *Freewill*

Family businesses are incredibly complex systems.
And because of this, many of the recommendations
and options laid out in this book might seem too
difficult or even impossible.

It certainly may seem easier to continue to plug
away, doing the same thing and hoping something
changes without taking any personal action or changing your mind-set. Make no mistake, though—taking no action is still making a decision.

You don't need to decide today what you will
do for the rest of your life. You don't need to decide tomorrow, next week, next month, or even next
year. But if you feel that this book was written for, or

about, you, even in part, you don't have much of an excuse not to take some action.

Whether it's merely starting a conversation, attending a workshop, or finding and talking to others trapped in their own family businesses, you owe it to yourself to do *something*.

As our careers progress, we should all be able to develop new skills and abilities as well as discover interests and passions we didn't know we possessed. Ultimately, our jobs and other professional experiences should guide us toward finding out where our true strengths and talents lay.

For many, the family business provides an unequalled arena for this type of professional development. Unfortunately, for far too many, the family business stands directly *in the way of this*—and, as a result, prevents normal, healthy adult development. And, ultimately, it keeps you from making the most out of your life.

GET IN TOUCH:

EMAIL
info@trappedinthefamilybusiness.com

FACEBOOK
facebook.com/trappedinthefamilybusiness/

TWITTER
@trappedinfambiz

EXPLORATION: KEY QUESTIONS

SECTION I: HISTORY

1. **When did you first work at the family business?**
2. **What was your role/responsibilities?**
3. **What other, if any, work options did you have?**

SECTION II: LEGACY

1. **What is the significance of this family business to you?**
2. **How important is it to you to continue being a part of this business? As an employee? As an owner?**
3. **Do you want this business to provide opportunities for your children (either for employment or ownership?) How important is that to you?**

SECTION III: RELATIONSHIPS

1. **Which familial relationships are most important to you?**
2. **Which, if any, are likely to be most impacted if you change roles or leave?**
3. **What would you like those relationships to look like in the short-term? Long-term?**

SECTION IV: CAREER

1. **Have you had other work experiences? What were they? What was a good fit about them? What wasn't?**
2. **What do you do in your current job that feels the most consistent with who you are, your strengths, and your values?**
3. **What are you hopes for looking back on a successful career?**

PROFESSIONAL RESOURCES

FAMILY BUSINESS CENTERS

These centers typically offer monthly or quarterly events for family business members on various topics, as well as provide groups focused on founders, CEOs, next-generation members, and other members of family businesses.

Locate a center in your region by Googling "family business center." Please note: many of these centers are based in universities (and are generally nonprofit), while others are privately run consulting or advisory firms. Therefore, some have a primarily educational approach, while others are sales or commercially oriented.

CAREER COUNSELORS & CONSULTANTS

These professionals are uniquely qualified to provide assistance in areas such as job fit, values and leadership assessment, resumes, interviewing preparation, and even how to best use social media for career development.

You can locate certified career professionals in your area by going to www.ncda.org and clicking on "Find a Counselor." You may also consider contacting your alma mater's alumni services career center for additional options.

PSYCHOLOGISTS

Most states prohibit use of the term "psychologist" unless you possess a state-issued license. The license guarantees that the provider has completed specific educational and testing requirements to offer services to the public.

Practicing psychologists typically specialize in counseling, therapy, and psychological assessment. Consider interviewing several candidates to assess your comfort level with them. This can be done initially over the phone, but many offer an exploratory face-to-face meeting to assess whether there is a fit between what they can provide and what a potential client is looking for (including "goodness of fit"— i.e., do you both believe you can work together?).

To find a licensed psychologist near you: http://locator.apa.org

BUSINESS ADVISORY BOARDS

These organizations bring together owners, CEOs, professionals, and other members of various size organizations in small groups to provide one another with insight, advice, and solutions for business problems.

While these groups are not designed specifically for family businesses and related issues, each group is different, and you may be able to find one in your area that consists primarily of family business members from other industries.

The following websites can provide you with information about groups that may meet in your region and information on specific group leaders. Attending these meetings (combined with one-to-one coaching from the group leader) can result in having numerous practical and helpful perspectives to consider.

You may want to interview the local team leader in depth and attend at least two or more meetings before making any decisions about membership.

- Vistage
  www.vistage.com
- The Alternative Board (TAB)
  www.thealternativeboard.com
- Young Presidents' Organization (YPO)
  www.ypo.org

VIDEO

Animated:

- *Coco*
- *Brave*
- *Kung Fu Panda*
- *Moana*

Films:

- *All Good Things*
- *The Godfather* series
- *Avalon*
- *BarberShop*
- *Family Business*
- *Indiana Jones and the Last Crusade*
- *Match Point*
- *The Mosquito Coast*

Television:

- *Arrested Development*
- *Brothers and Sisters*
- *Six Feet Under*
- *The Sopranos*

PRINT

Family Business Magazine
www.familybusinessmagazine.com

When Your Parents Sign the Paychecks: Finding Career Success Inside or Outside the Family Business, by Greg McCann, 2007.

Family Wars: The Real Stories behind the Most Famous Family Business Feuds, by Grant Gordon and Nigel Nicholson, 2010.

Family Business on the Couch: A Psychological Perspective, by Manfred F. R. Kets de Vries, Randel S. Carlock, Elizabeth Florent-Treacy, 2007.

What Color Is Your Parachute? A Practical Manual for Job-Hunters and Career-Changers, by Richard N. Bolles (updated annually).

68642728R00087

Made in the USA
Columbia, SC
11 August 2019